Animal Top Tens

The Polar Regions' Most Amazing Animals

Anita Ganeri

www.raintreepublishers.co.uk
Visit our website to find out more information about Raintree books.

To order:
☎ Phone 44 (0) 1865 888112
▤ Send a fax to 44 (0) 1865 314091
▯ Visit the Raintree Bookshop at **www.raintreepublishers.co.uk** to browse our catalogue and order online

First published in Great Britain by Raintree,
Halley Court, Jordan Hill, Oxford OX2 8EJ, part of
Harcourt Education.
Raintree is a registered trademark of Harcourt
Education Ltd.

Editorial: Nancy Dickmann and Catherine Veitch
Design: Victoria Bevan and Geoff Ward
Illustrations: Geoff Ward
Picture Research: Mica Brancic
Production: Victoria Fitzgerald

Originated by Modern Age
Printed and bound by CTPS (China Translation
& Printing Services Ltd)

13-digit ISBN 978 1 4062 0921 1
12 11 10 09 08
10 9 8 7 6 5 4 3 2 1

British Library Cataloguing in Publication Data
Ganeri, Anita, 1961-
   The Polar Regions' Most Amazing Animals. - (Animal
top tens)
   591.7'586
A full catalogue record for this book is available from the
British Library.

Acknowledgements
The author and publisher are grateful to the following
for permission to reproduce copyright material: ©Ardea
pp. **4** (Jean-Paul Ferrero), **9** (Doc White), **18** (François
Gohier), **19** (Jean-Paul Ferrero), **22** (Graham Robertson)
[FLPA], **24** (Bob Gibbons), **26** (John Swedberg); ©FLPA
pp. **12, 20, 23, 25**; ©FLPA/Minden Pictures pp. **7, 8,
10, 13, 14, 15, 21**; ©Getty Images/National Geographic
p. **16–17** (Bill Curtsinger), **27** (Paul Sutherland);
photolibrary.com p. **11**; Robyn Stewart/ardea.com p. **6**.

Cover photograph of an Arctic fox with its winter
coat, reproduced with permission of osf.co.uk/
Norbert Rosing.

The publishers would like to thank Michael Bright for
his assistance with the preparation of this book.

Every effort has been made to contact copyright holders
of any material reproduced in this book. Any omissions
will be rectified in subsequent printings if notice is given
to the publishers.

Contents

Some words are printed in bold, **like this**. You can find out what they mean on page 31 in the Glossary.

The Polar Regions

The **polar** regions lie at the north and south ends of the Earth. The region around the North Pole is called the Arctic. The region around the South Pole is called the Antarctic, or Antarctica. The Arctic region is made up of the Arctic Ocean, which is frozen over for most of the year, and the land around it. Antarctica is a huge **continent** of land, covered with an enormous sheet of ice. Mountains and **volcanoes** are buried underneath the ice.

The Poles are the coldest places on Earth. In the Arctic, the temperatures fall to below -40 °C (-40 °F) in winter. Antarctica is even colder, with winter temperatures of -60 °C (-76 °F).

The polar regions are the coldest, driest and windiest places on Earth.

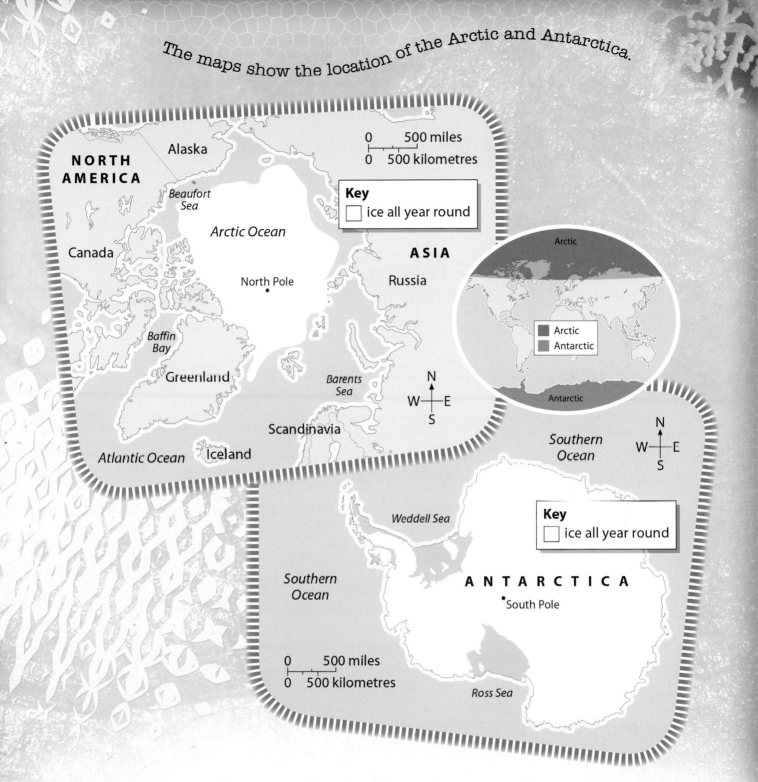

The maps show the location of the Arctic and Antarctica.

NORTH AMERICA

Alaska

Beaufort Sea

Arctic Ocean

Canada

North Pole

Baffin Bay

Greenland

Scandinavia

Atlantic Ocean

Iceland

Barents Sea

ASIA

Russia

0 500 miles
0 500 kilometres

Key
☐ ice all year round

N
W E
S

Arctic

Arctic
Antarctic

Antarctic

Southern Ocean

N
W E
S

Weddell Sea

Key
☐ ice all year round

ANTARCTICA

South Pole

Southern Ocean

0 500 miles
0 500 kilometres

Ross Sea

Despite the cold, wind and ice, a large number of animals are able to live at the Poles. They have special features and ways of behaving to help them survive. They live on the ice, on the land, around the coasts and in the icy polar seas.

Polar bear

The polar bear is the largest type of bear. It is also the biggest meat-eating animal and **mammal** on land. It lives around the coast of the Arctic Ocean. The polar bear mainly hunts ringed seals to eat.

POLAR BEAR

BODY LENGTH:
UP TO 2.6 M (8.5 FT)

HEIGHT AT SHOULDER:
UP TO 1.6 M (5.2 FT)

WEIGHT:
UP TO 800 KG (1760 LBS)

LIFESPAN:
15–18 YEARS

HABITAT:
ARCTIC COASTS AND SEA ICE

THAT'S AMAZING!:
POLAR BEARS HAVE A BRILLIANT SENSE OF SMELL. THEY CAN SNIFF OUT A SEAL OR A DEAD WHALE OR WALRUS ON THE ICE FROM OVER 1 KM (0.62 MILES) AWAY.

where polar bears live

Russia

Arctic Ocean

Greenland

Canada

Polar bears hunt for seals on the ice, looking for breathing holes.

Polar bears paddle with their front feet, using their back legs to steer.

Bear features

Polar bears are very well-**adapted** for their Arctic life, with thick fur to keep them warm. Their fur looks creamy-white which makes them difficult to see on the ice. A thick layer of **blubber** under their skin gives them extra warmth. They have small bumps on their feet and long hairs between their toes to help them grip the ice.

Beluga

Belugas are whales that live in the Arctic Ocean and the seas around it. They dive underwater to hunt fish, squid, and **seabed** animals, such as crabs and snails.

BELUGA

BODY LENGTH:
3–5 M (9.8–16.4 FT)

WEIGHT:
0.5–1.5 TONNES
(0.55–1.65 TONS)

LIFESPAN:
25–30 YEARS

HABITAT:
ARCTIC OCEAN AND
SURROUNDING SEAS

THAT'S AMAZING!:
TO STAY WARM IN THE FREEZING SEA, BELUGAS HAVE A THICK LAYER OF **BLUBBER** UNDER THEIR SKIN.

where belugas live

Russia

Arctic Ocean

Greenland

Canada

About 10 belugas live together in pods or groups. Sometimes these groups join to form much larger groups.

Sound senses

It can often be difficult for animals and fish to see where they are going in the dark sea water. Belugas **navigate** and find food using sound. They make lots of quick, clicking sounds. The sounds hit objects in the water and send back **echoes**. This is called echo-location.

From these echoes, belugas find out the size, shape, speed, and location of objects. Belugas also use echo-location to find breathing holes in the ice when the ocean is frozen over.

Newborn belugas are brown. They turn white as they grow up.

Arctic fox

The Arctic fox is a **mammal**. It feeds mostly on other smaller mammals, such as lemmings and voles. In winter, it uses its excellent hearing to listen for creatures under the snow. Then it jumps up and down on the ground, breaks open a hole with its paws, and grabs its **prey**.

The tundra

The icy land around the Arctic Ocean is called the tundra. Beneath the surface, the ground is always frozen but in summer, the top few centimetres melt. Some low-growing plants, such as mosses and lichens, live on the tundra.

In winter, the Arctic fox can survive in temperatures as low as -50 °C (-58 °F).

Changing colour

In summer, the Arctic fox grows a grey-brown coat so it can hide among the **tundra** rocks. In winter, it grows a white coat so it can hide in the snow. These changes give the fox good **camouflage** all year round.

ARCTIC FOX

BODY LENGTH:
50–70 CM (19.5–27.3 IN)

TAIL LENGTH:
28–40 CM (10.9–15.6 IN)

WEIGHT:
2.5–8 KG (5.5–17.6 LBS)

LIFESPAN:
3–6 YEARS

HABITAT:
ARCTIC TUNDRA

THAT'S AMAZING!:
ARCTIC FOXES SOMETIMES FOLLOW POLAR BEARS ONTO THE SEA ICE, LOOKING FOR SCRAPS FROM THEIR KILLS.

where Arctic foxes live

Russia

Arctic Ocean

Greenland

Canada

An Arctic fox in its grey-brown summer coat.

Arctic tern

The Arctic tern makes the longest **migration** of any bird. Every year it flies from the Arctic to Antarctica, and back again. Each year it spends eight months flying and covers around 40,000 kilometres (24,840 miles).

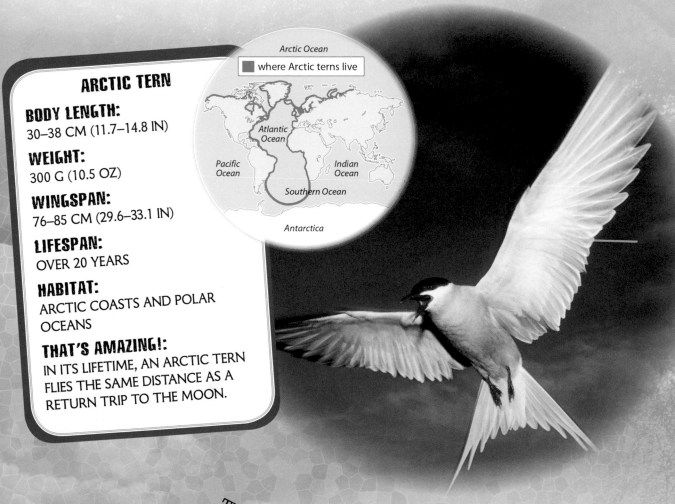

ARCTIC TERN

BODY LENGTH:
30–38 CM (11.7–14.8 IN)

WEIGHT:
300 G (10.5 OZ)

WINGSPAN:
76–85 CM (29.6–33.1 IN)

LIFESPAN:
OVER 20 YEARS

HABITAT:
ARCTIC COASTS AND POLAR OCEANS

THAT'S AMAZING!:
IN ITS LIFETIME, AN ARCTIC TERN FLIES THE SAME DISTANCE AS A RETURN TRIP TO THE MOON.

Arctic Ocean

■ where Arctic terns live

Atlantic Ocean

Pacific Ocean

Indian Ocean

Southern Ocean

Antarctica

The Arctic tern is a medium-sized black and white bird with a bright orange beak and forked tail.

A female tern lays 1–3 eggs in the grass.
Both parents guard their nest fiercely.

Migration
Many animals make long journeys between their breeding and feeding grounds. This is called migration. It lets them take advantage of the best weather and food supplies.

Two summers

The tern **breeds** around the Arctic Ocean during the Arctic summer. As winter comes it flies south to Antarctica. When it is winter in the Arctic it is summer in Antarctica. In Antarctica it feeds on the plentiful fish of the Southern Ocean.

Musk ox

The musk ox is one of the largest animals on the Arctic **tundra**. To help it live in the freezing cold it has very thick fur with two layers. The outer fur is rough and stiff, and lets the rain and snow slide off easily. Underneath is a layer of soft, thick fur which gives the ox extra warmth.

The musk ox's shaggy coat almost reaches to the ground.

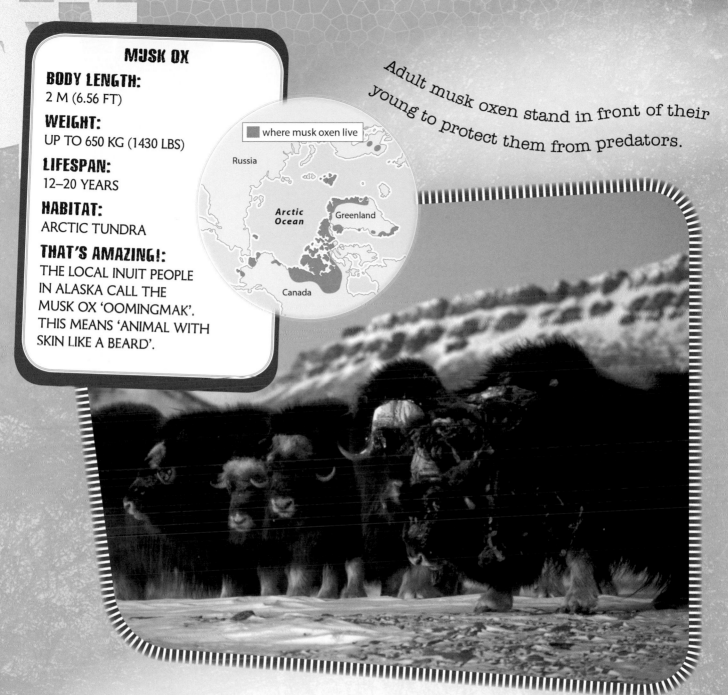

MUSK OX

BODY LENGTH:
2 M (6.56 FT)

WEIGHT:
UP TO 650 KG (1430 LBS)

LIFESPAN:
12–20 YEARS

HABITAT:
ARCTIC TUNDRA

THAT'S AMAZING!:
THE LOCAL INUIT PEOPLE IN ALASKA CALL THE MUSK OX 'OOMINGMAK'. THIS MEANS 'ANIMAL WITH SKIN LIKE A BEARD'.

where musk oxen live

Russia

Arctic
Ocean

Greenland

Canada

Adult musk oxen stand in front of their young to protect them from predators.

Keeping safe

Musk oxen live in large herds of 15-20 animals. If a wolf attacks, the musk oxen stand in a circle and face outwards. The young musk oxen hide behind the adults for safety. If the wolf comes closer, the musk oxen charge with their long, curved horns.

Antarctic cod

The Antarctic cod lives in the freezing cold water around the Antarctic coast. It swims near the bottom of the sea and its eyes have **adapted** to be able to see in the dark water underneath the ice. The Antarctic cod mostly feeds on other fish but will also eat the remains of penguins killed by seals. It has strong jaws which are lined with inward pointing teeth. The fish uses its teeth to catch and keep hold of **prey**. It is also called the Antarctic toothfish.

The Antarctic cod is a very large, olive-green coloured fish. It has a broad head and narrow body.

Antifreeze blood

Most fish would not be able to survive in the freezing Southern Ocean. Their bodies would freeze and they would die. But the Antarctic cod has a chemical, like antifreeze, in its body which stops ice crystals growing in its blood.

ANTARCTIC COD

BODY LENGTH:
UP TO 1.75 M (5.7 FT)

WEIGHT:
80 KG (176 LBS)

LIFESPAN:
UP TO 30 YEARS

HABITAT:
SOUTHERN OCEAN

THAT'S AMAZING!:
SCIENTISTS TRYING TO FIND OUT MORE ABOUT ANTARCTIC COD FIT SPECIAL TAGS TO THE BODIES OF THE FISH. SIGNALS FROM THE TAGS ARE PICKED UP BY UNDERWATER MICROPHONES.

where Antarctic cod live

Weddell Sea

Antarctica

Ross Sea

Southern Ocean

Blue whale

The gigantic blue whale is the largest animal in the world. Scientists think it is the largest that has ever lived. It lives in oceans all over the world, including the Southern Ocean around Antarctica.

Under a blue whale's skin there is a thick layer of **blubber** to keep it warm in the cold sea.

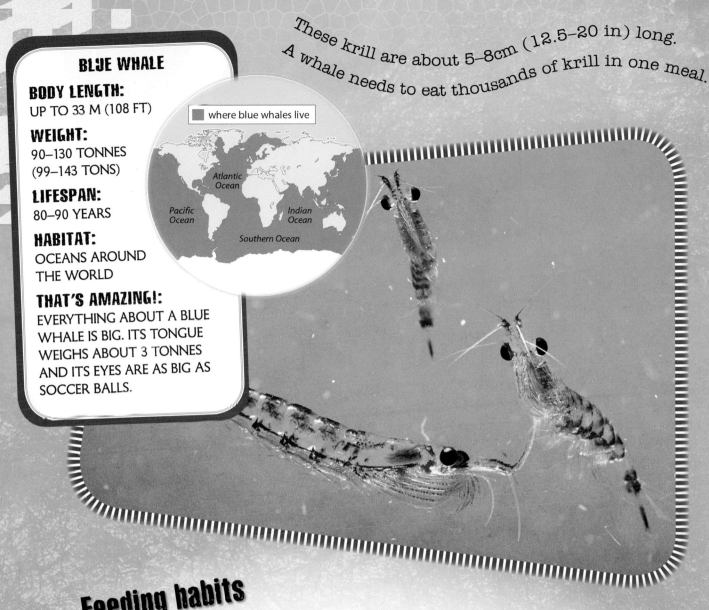

BLUE WHALE

BODY LENGTH:
UP TO 33 M (108 FT)

WEIGHT:
90–130 TONNES
(99–143 TONS)

LIFESPAN:
80–90 YEARS

HABITAT:
OCEANS AROUND
THE WORLD

THAT'S AMAZING!:
EVERYTHING ABOUT A BLUE
WHALE IS BIG. ITS TONGUE
WEIGHS ABOUT 3 TONNES
AND ITS EYES ARE AS BIG AS
SOCCER BALLS.

where blue whales live

Atlantic
Ocean

Pacific
Ocean

Indian
Ocean

Southern Ocean

Feeding habits

After **breeding** in warmer seas, blue whales move to polar
seas in the summer. At this time, the Southern Ocean is
rich in krill, the whale's main food. A whale can eat 4 tonnes
(4.4 tons) of krill in one day. The whale has giant plates,
called baleen, hanging down from its top jaw. As it swims,
it gulps in huge mouthfuls of water and krill. Then it
pushes the water out through its baleen and swallows
the krill. The baleen acts like an enormous sieve.

Weddell seal

The Weddell seal lives in Antarctica, further south than any other seal. It spends most of its time in the icy-cold water, living under several metres of ice. The Weddell seal has a layer of **blubber** under its skin. The blubber keeps it warm in the freezing water. The blubber is very thick and makes up a large part of its body weight.

Weddell seals pull themselves on to the ice to rest and have their pups.

WEDDELL SEAL

BODY LENGTH:
3 M (9.8 FT)

WEIGHT:
UP TO 450 KG (990 LBS)

LIFESPAN:
UP TO 30 YEARS

HABITAT:
ANTARCTIC SEA ICE
AND ISLANDS

THAT'S AMAZING!:
EVENTUALLY THE TEETH
OF THE WEDDELL SEAL GET
WORN DOWN FROM GNAWING
THROUGH THE ICE. THIS MEANS
THEY CAN'T GNAW OUT
BREATHING HOLES AND THEY
DROWN IN THE WATER.

where Weddell seals live

Weddell
Sea

Antarctica

Ross
Sea

SouthernOcean

Weddell seals have smooth bodies and flippers for swimming.

Deep diver

Weddell seals dive underwater to feed on squid and fish.
They can hold their breath for up to 45 minutes but then
need to surface to breathe. If there are no cracks in the ice,
they gnaw out a breathing hole with their large front teeth.

Emperor penguin

The Emperor penguin is the largest type of penguin. It feeds on fish and squid which it catches out at sea. Its body is **adapted** for swimming and keeping warm. It uses its wings as flippers and its tail for steering. Its short, thick feathers are windproof and waterproof. A layer of **blubber** underneath its skin keeps the penguin warm.

The male tucks the egg under a warm flap of skin.

EMPEROR PENGUIN

BODY LENGTH:
UP TO 115 CM
(3.7 FT)

WEIGHT:
20–45 KG
(44–99 LBS)

LIFESPAN:
20 YEARS

HABITAT:
ANTARCTIC SEA
ICE AND COAST

THAT'S AMAZING!:
EMPEROR PENGUINS HAVE
KNOBBLY BUMPS ON THEIR
MOUTHS AND TONGUES
TO STOP FISH AND SQUID
WRIGGLING AWAY.

where Emperor penguins live

Weddell Sea

Antarctica

Ross Sea

Southern Ocean

The penguins take turns moving to the inside of the group, where it is warmer.

Winter breeders

Emperor penguins **breed** on the ice in mid-winter. The female lays an egg and then goes off to sea to feed. The male carries the egg on his feet. For the next two months he looks after the egg. To keep warm in the freezing temperatures he huddles together in a group with thousands of other male penguins. The female returns as the chick is about to hatch. Then, the male goes into the sea to feed.

Wandering albatross

The wandering albatross has the longest wingspan of any bird. It uses its wings to **soar** over the Southern Ocean searching for fish and squid that are near the surface. It scoops its **prey** from the water with its large, hooked bill.

WANDERING ALBATROSS

BODY LENGTH:
1.3 M (4.4 FT)

WINGSPAN:
UP TO 3.5 M (11.4 FT)

WEIGHT:
6–12 KG
(13.2–26.4 LBS)

LIFESPAN:
UP TO 60 YEARS

HABITAT:
SOUTHERN OCEAN

THAT'S AMAZING!:
AN ALBATROSS CAN 'LOCK' ITS WINGS IN POSITION SO THAT IT CAN KEEP THEM STRETCHED OUT WITHOUT GETTING UNCOMFORTABLE.

Arctic Ocean

where wandering albatrosses live

Atlantic Ocean

Pacific Ocean

Indian Ocean

Southern Ocean

Albatrosses sometimes follow fishing boats and pick up scraps of fish.

Nests and chicks

Albatrosses spend most of their time in the air and only **breed** or feed on land. They build cone-shaped nests on islands and lay one egg inside. The egg hatches after two months, but the chick does not leave its nest for another ten months.

The parents take turns bringing food for the chick.

Wing shapes

To save energy, the wandering albatross hardly ever flaps its wings. Instead, it glides on **air currents** rising up off the sea. Its long, pointed wings are shaped for soaring.

Animals in danger

Many kinds of **polar** animals are in danger of dying out forever. When this happens an animal is said to be **extinct**. Human activities, such as mining, drilling for oil and overfishing, are harming the polar regions. Scientists also think that **global warming** may be melting the polar ice.

This pipeline carries oil through Alaska. Drilling for oil is putting wildlife in serious danger.

The Arctic National Wildlife Refuge covers a huge area of Alaska, USA. It is home to many Arctic animals, including caribou, polar bears, and Arctic foxes. Scientists are worried about plans to drill for oil in the area. Roads, pipelines, airstrips, and power stations will have to be built and this will damage the amazing **habitat** forever.

The polar oceans are rich in fish, squid, and krill. Millions of tonnes are caught each year by fishing fleets. To prevent overfishing, there are strict rules about how many fish can be taken. But some fleets are breaking the rules. In the Southern Ocean, huge numbers of Patagonian toothfish (also known as Chilean sea bass) are being caught **illegally**.

Animal facts and figures

There are millions of different kinds of animals living all over the world. The place where an animal lives is called its **habitat**. Animals have special features, such as wings, claws, and fins. These features allow animals to survive in their habitats. Which animal do you think is the most amazing?

POLAR BEAR

BODY LENGTH:
UP TO 2.6 M (8.5 FT)

HEIGHT AT SHOULDER:
UP TO 1.6 M (5.2 FT)

WEIGHT:
UP TO 800 KG (1760 LBS)

LIFESPAN:
15–18 YEARS

HABITAT:
ARCTIC COASTS AND SEA ICE

THAT'S AMAZING!:
POLAR BEARS HAVE A BRILLIANT SENSE OF SMELL. THEY CAN SNIFF OUT A SEAL OR A DEAD WHALE OR WALRUS ON THE ICE FROM OVER 1 KM (0.62 MILES) AWAY.

BELUGA

BODY LENGTH:
3–5 M (9.8–16.4 FT)

WEIGHT:
0.5–1.5 TONNES (0.55–1.65 TONS)

LIFESPAN:
25–30 YEARS

HABITAT:
ARCTIC OCEAN AND SURROUNDING SEAS

THAT'S AMAZING!:
TO STAY WARM IN THE FREEZING SEA, BELUGAS HAVE A THICK LAYER OF **BLUBBER** UNDER THEIR SKIN.

ARCTIC FOX

BODY LENGTH:
50–70 CM (19.5–27.3 IN)

TAIL LENGTH:
28–40 CM (10.9–15.6 IN)

WEIGHT:
2.5–8 KG (5.5–17.6 LBS)

LIFESPAN:
3–6 YEARS

HABITAT:
ARCTIC **TUNDRA**

THAT'S AMAZING!:
ARCTIC FOXES SOMETIMES FOLLOW POLAR BEARS ONTO THE SEA ICE, LOOKING FOR SCRAPS FROM THEIR KILLS.

ARCTIC TERN

BODY LENGTH:
30–38 CM (11.7–14.8 IN)

WEIGHT:
300 G (10.5 OZ)

WINGSPAN:
76–85 CM (29.6–33.1 IN)

LIFESPAN:
OVER 20 YEARS

HABITAT:
ARCTIC COASTS AND POLAR OCEANS

THAT'S AMAZING!:
IN ITS LIFETIME, AN ARCTIC TERN FLIES THE SAME DISTANCE AS A RETURN TRIP TO THE MOON.

MUSK OX

BODY LENGTH:
2 M (6.56 FT)

WEIGHT:
UP TO 650 KG (1430 LBS)

LIFESPAN:
12–20 YEARS

HABITAT:
ARCTIC TUNDRA

THAT'S AMAZING!:
THE LOCAL INUIT PEOPLE IN ALASKA CALL THE MUSK OX 'OOMINGMAK'. THIS MEANS 'ANIMAL WITH SKIN LIKE A BEARD'.

ANTARCTIC COD

BODY LENGTH:
UP TO 1.75 M (5.7 FT)

WEIGHT:
80 KG (176 LBS)

LIFESPAN:
UP TO 30 YEARS

HABITAT:
SOUTHERN OCEAN

THAT'S AMAZING!:
SCIENTISTS TRYING TO FIND OUT MORE ABOUT ANTARCTIC COD FIT SPECIAL TAGS TO THE BODIES OF THE FISH. SIGNALS FROM THE TAGS ARE PICKED UP BY UNDERWATER MICROPHONES.

BLUE WHALE

BODY LENGTH:
UP TO 33 M (108 FT)

WEIGHT:
90–130 TONNES (99–143 TONS)

LIFESPAN:
80–90 YEARS

HABITAT:
OCEANS AROUND THE WORLD

THAT'S AMAZING!:
EVERYTHING ABOUT A BLUE WHALE IS BIG. ITS TONGUE WEIGHS ABOUT 3 TONNES AND ITS EYES ARE AS BIG AS SOCCER BALLS.

WEDDELL SEAL

BODY HEIGHT:
3 M (9.8 FT)

WEIGHT:
UP TO 450 KG (990 LBS)

LIFESPAN:
UP TO 30 YEARS

HABITAT:
ANTARCTIC SEA ICE AND ISLANDS

THAT'S AMAZING!:
EVENTUALLY THE TEETH OF THE WEDDELL SEAL GET WORN DOWN FROM GNAWING THROUGH THE ICE. THIS MEANS THEY CAN'T GNAW OUT BREATHING HOLES AND THEY DROWN IN THE WATER.

EMPEROR PENGUIN

BODY LENGTH:
UP TO 115 CM (3.7 FT)

WEIGHT:
20–45 KG (44–99 LBS)

LIFESPAN:
20 YEARS

HABITAT:
ANTARCTIC SEA ICE AND COAST

THAT'S AMAZING!:
EMPEROR PENGUINS HAVE KNOBBLY BUMPS ON THEIR MOUTHS AND TONGUES TO STOP FISH AND SQUID WRIGGLING AWAY.

WANDERING ALBATROSS

BODY LENGTH:
1.3 M (4.4 FT)

WINGSPAN:
UP TO 3.5 M (11.4 FT)

WEIGHT:
6–12 KG (13.2–26.4 LBS)

LIFESPAN:
UP TO 60 YEARS

HABITAT:
SOUTHERN OCEAN

THAT'S AMAZING!:
AN ALBATROSS CAN 'LOCK' ITS WINGS IN POSITION SO THAT IT CAN KEEP THEM STRETCHED OUT WITHOUT GETTING UNCOMFORTABLE.

Find out more

Books to read

Exploring Continents: Antarctica, Tristan Boyer Binns (Heinemann Library, 2007)

Living Things: Adaptation, Holly Wallace (Heinemann Library, 2001)

Living Things: Survival and Change, Holly Wallace (Heinemann Library, 2001)

Websites

http://www.bbc.co.uk/nature/reallywild
Type in the name of the animal you want to learn about and find a page with lots of facts, figures, and pictures.

http://animals.nationalgeographic.com/animals
This site has information on the different groups of animals, stories of survival in different habitats, and stunning photo galleries to search through.

http://animaldiversity.ummz.umich.edu
A website run by the University of Michigan which has a huge encyclopedia of animals to search through.

http://www.mnh.si.edu
The website of the Smithsonian National Museum of Natural History, which has one of the largest natural history collections in the world.

Zoo sites
Many zoos around the world have their own websites which tell you about the animals they keep, where they come from, and how they are looked after.

Glossary

adapted when an animal has special features that help it to survive in its habitat

air current stream of air that rises upwards

blubber thick layer of fat underneath an animal's skin

breed when an animal makes babies with another animal

camouflage when an animal has special colours or markings which help it hide in its habitat

continent one of seven huge pieces of land on Earth. Each continent is divided into smaller regions called countries.

echo sound that is heard again when it bounces off something

extinct when a kind of animal dies out forever

global warming how the Earth is getting warmer because of gases put into the air

habitat place where an animal lives and feeds

illegally something that is done without permission or is against the law

lichen living thing that is a fungus and an alga (tiny plant) living together

mammal animal that has fur or hair and feeds its babies on milk

migration long journey made by some animals to find a better place to breed or feed in

navigate find the way

polar describes areas around the North and South Poles

prey animals that are hunted and killed by other animals for food

seabed muddy, rocky, or sandy bottom of the sea

soar when a bird flies through the air without flapping its wings

tundra cold, icy land around the Arctic Ocean

volcano mountain that can erupt (explode), shooting out red-hot rocks and ash

Index